HAL•LEONARD
INSTRUMENTAL
PLAY-ALONG

AUDIO
ACCESS
INCLUDED

PLAYBACK+
Speed • Pitch • Balance • Loop

FLUTE

WEST SIDE STORY®

Based on a conception of Jerome Robbins

Book by
Arthur Laurents

Music by
Leonard Bernstein®

Lyrics by
Stephen Sondheim

Entire Original Production
Directed and Choreographed by
Jerome Robbins

ISBN 978-1-4234-5823-4

To access companion recorded audio, visit:
www.halleonard.com/mylibrary

Enter Code
1905-2228-9176-6222

LEONARD
BERNSTEIN
Music Publishing
Company LLC

BOOSEY & HAWKES

DISTRIBUTED BY

HAL•LEONARD®

Visit Hal Leonard Online at
www.halleonard.com

Contact us:
Hal Leonard
7777 West Bluemound Road
Milwaukee, WI 53213
Email: info@halleonard.com

In Europe, contact:
Hal Leonard Europe Limited
42 Wigmore Street
Marylebone, London, W1U 2RN
Email: info@halleonardeurope.com

In Australia, contact:
Hal Leonard Australia Pty. Ltd.
4 Lentara Court
Cheltenham, Victoria, 3192 Australia
Email: info@halleonard.com.au

CONTENTS

The price of this publication includes access to companion recorded audio online, for download or streaming, using the unique code found on the title page. Visit **www.halleonard.com/mylibrary** and enter the access code.

A melody cue is included on the right channel only which may be adjusted up or down to hear the accompaniment or full version.

◆ AMERICA

Flute

Lyrics by STEPHEN SONDHEIM
Music by LEONARD BERNSTEIN

❷ COOL

FLUTE

Lyrics by STEPHEN SONDHEIM
Music by LEONARD BERNSTEIN

◆3 I FEEL PRETTY

Flute

Lyrics by STEPHEN SONDHEIM
Music by LEONARD BERNSTEIN

I HAVE A LOVE

FLUTE

Lyrics by STEPHEN SONDHEIM
Music by LEONARD BERNSTEIN

◆ JET SONG

Flute

Lyrics by STEPHEN SONDHEIM
Music by LEONARD BERNSTEIN

◆ MARIA

FLUTE

Lyrics by STEPHEN SONDHEIM
Music by LEONARD BERNSTEIN

❖ ONE HAND, ONE HEART

Flute

Lyrics by STEPHEN SONDHEIM
Music by LEONARD BERNSTEIN

◆ 8 SOMETHING'S COMING

FLUTE

Lyrics by STEPHEN SONDHEIM
Music by LEONARD BERNSTEIN

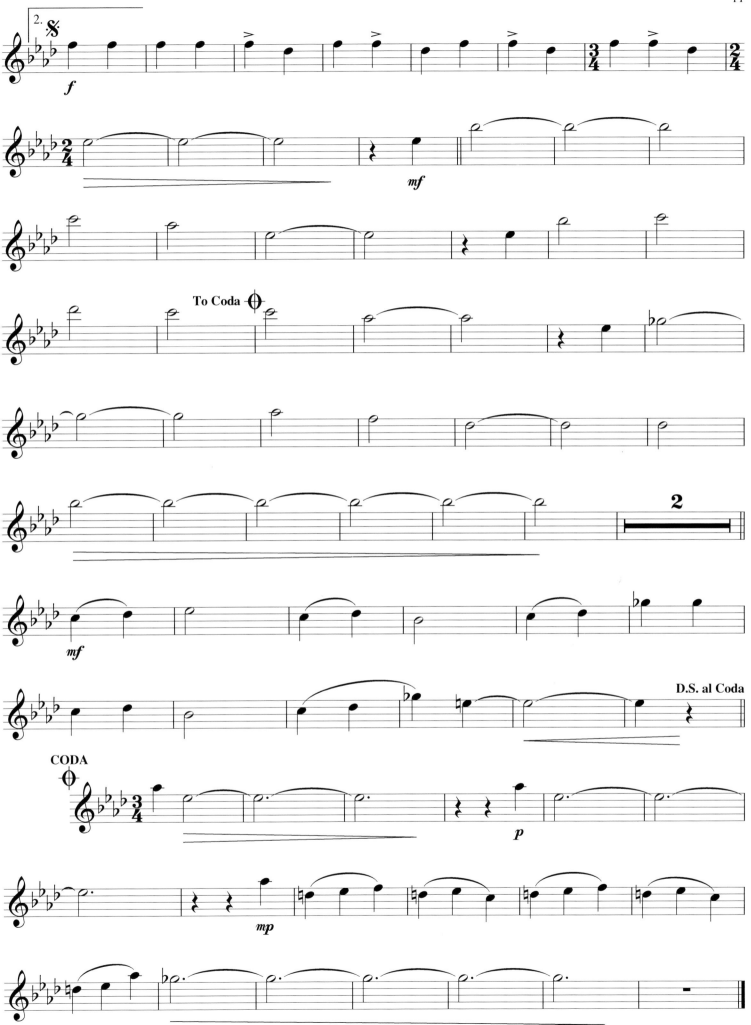

◆ ⑨ SOMEWHERE

FLUTE

Lyrics by STEPHEN SONDHEIM
Music by LEONARD BERNSTEIN

TONIGHT

FLUTE

Lyrics by STEPHEN SONDHEIM
Music by LEONARD BERNSTEIN